COSMIC
MOMENTS

Books By Ron Scolastico

YOUR SPIRITUAL TEMPLE: Being a Soul in a Physical Body
Retreat Series, Volume 1
THE HEALING POWER OF JOY: A Spiritual Perspective
Retreat Series, Volume 2
THE MAGIC OF CREATIVITY: A Spiritual Power
Retreat Series, Volume 3

BECOMING ENLIGHTENED
Twelve Keys to Higher Consciousness

THE MYSTERY OF THE CHRIST FORCE
A Personal Story of Enlightenment
for Spiritual Seekers

DOORWAY TO THE SOUL
How to Have a Profound Spiritual Experience

REFLECTIONS
Inspired Wisdom on: Gods and Symbols;
The Human Mind; Angels and Guides; Education;
Healing Addictions; and, Healing the Hurt Child

HEALING THE HEART,
HEALING THE BODY
A Spiritual Perspective on Emotional,
Mental, and Physical Health

THE EARTH ADVENTURE
Your Soul's Journey Through Physical Reality

COSMIC MOMENTS

Inspiring Reminders Of Your Eternal Nature

༐

Ron Scolastico, Ph.D.
Compiled by Susan Scolastico

UNIVERSAL GUIDANCE PRESS

COSMIC MOMENTS

Inspiring Reminders of Your Eternal Nature

UNIVERSAL GUIDANCE PRESS

Woodland Hills, California

www.ronscolastico.com

1-818-224-4488

For my wife, Susan Scolastico,
who has continually inspired me,
and who contributed so much
to the creation of this book.

Contents

Contents

Contents

Contents

Contents

Contents

Contents

Contents

Contents

PART ONE

HOW TO USE
THIS BOOK

How to Use This Book

———— ✳ ————

*A*s a spiritual seeker, you know that the complexity and chaos of the physical world can at times make it difficult to turn your attention to the true spiritual nature of life. From my years of work as a spiritual counselor to many people, it has become clear to me that spiritual seekers need ways to help them remember who they are as eternal beings living a temporary life in a physical world.

The most effective way to awaken to your eternal nature is to have an ongoing spiritual practice that you do every day, such as meditation, prayer, Yoga, Tai Chi, a spiritual communion with nature, or other such focal points. Yet, many people who have such a focus tell me that they often lose the inspiration that they gain from their spiritual practice when they go out into the world to cope with the realities of a demanding society. Also, they say that it is difficult to stay inspired when they feel discouraged or frightened from their constant exposure to

19

daily news reports of disasters and tragedies that occur around the world.

Others who do not have a spiritual practice tell me that they are so busy earning a living and making their way in the world that they just do not have the time to meditate, or drive to a Yoga class, or commune with nature.

In my work, I have discovered that, no matter what a person's life situation might be, no matter how busy their days are, they can learn to create at least a brief moment of spiritual experience in their daily life. This means that *you* can create such spiritual moments. And, with practice, those brief moments can come to be very deep and very inspiring. In time, they can become *cosmic moments* that awaken you to the magnificent spiritual realities of life.

❖

I have written this book to help spiritual seekers achieve those inspirational moments, no matter where they go, or what they need to do in the world. Drawing upon more than forty years of spiritual work with individuals, and my own deep experiences of expanded consciousness, I have prepared a series of powerful daily statements that can help you awaken to your eternal nature as a soul.

I call these statements *reminders*. I use the word, "reminder," because I believe that within each of us, hidden beneath our conscious awareness, there is already an intuitive knowing of the spiritual truths of life. We simply need to be reminded of those truths so that they can be brought forward to become part of our conscious awareness.

❖

The reminders in Part Two present powerful ideas and inspiring statements that you can first *think* about in a deep way. Then, as you use the statements day after day, you can begin to *feel* the underlying spiritual realities that the words are describing. Using these reminders consistently over a period of time can help you awaken your ability to experience the majesty of the spiritual realities that sustain your being.

❖

Each page gives you a different important reminder. Some of the statements are focused on the underlying spiritual realities that seekers have investigated throughout the ages—the all-loving Creative Source of life; the Divine Universal Consciousness of which we are all a part; the eternal Oneness of life; or, what some people think of as God. There are also some reminders that offer effective ways to work with your thoughts, feelings, and actions in daily life to help you create the fulfillment that you desire.

Most of the reminders present complete ideas that you can absorb and quickly understand. A few of them are intentionally enticing. They are designed to stimulate *initial* thoughts in your mind, and then give you the opportunity to expand on those thoughts in your own way. With those reminders, you can complete the ideas for yourself.

You will notice that some of the reminders address a similar theme, but they each approach it from a different angle. That is because my experience has shown that these are very important themes and we all need more practice with them on a daily basis.

❖

An effective way to use these reminders is to choose one to work with for a full day. In the morning, before you go out into your activities in the world, read your chosen reminder with a sensitivity to the *thoughts* that it stimulates in you. For a few minutes, think deeply about the content of the statement.

Next, shift to your *feelings*. Invite yourself to feel deeply moved, or comforted, or inspired, or to have some other strong positive feeling that is stimulated by the thoughts that you are having about the reminder that you just read.

In this way, you can create a spiritual moment that will help you begin your day with *inspiration*, rather than beginning with thoughts about the complexities and challenges of the world that you must deal with in the coming day.

Then, during your day, re-read your chosen reminder. Allow it to stimulate thoughts and feelings of inspiration as often as you desire throughout the day. That will help you create calming, loving feelings to balance the intensity of your ordinary thoughts and feelings that are associated with the many pressing details of your life in the physical world.

❖

In working with the statements, you might choose to begin with the first one for a day, and then each day move on to the next reminder.

Or, you may choose to simply open the book at random each day and work with the reminder on that page, trusting that it will be the right inspiration for that day.

If you particularly like a certain reminder, finding it especially meaningful and inspiring, then work with that same one for several days.

Use your creativity to go through the book in the way that is most helpful for you. The important thing is to open yourself to inspiration throughout each day, using the reminders as a catalyst for awakening yourself to the deeper truths of life, and for remembering who you are as a spiritual being.

❖

The process of discovering your eternal nature can enrich every day of your journey through life. It can become a journey of greater joy, love, and exciting fulfillment. As you awaken to the true majesty of your being, that experience can make even the most ordinary moment a cosmic moment.

❖ ❖ ❖

PART TWO

REMINDERS
OF YOUR
ETERNAL NATURE

Creation And You

*W*oven into the very fabric of the physical world is an extraordinary *all-pervasive, illuminating love energy.* That perfect, magnificent energy is the cause of all creation. It is *the Divine experience of unending love,* or *God,* that sustains your being.

৯৫

A Personal Quest

*A*s a sincere seeker, you are on a *personal* quest. No matter what your beliefs, philosophy, or religion might be, and no matter what group you might belong to, an important aspect of your quest is to discover that: *There is no distance between you and the extraordinary Divine Forces of God.* There is no *time*, there is no *space* that can separate you from Divine Love.

৯৹৶

The Eternal You

*F*rom the beginning of time, *you* have existed. Your present human life is a journey through which you can discover the *you* that has been expressing as a *soul* through many lifetimes on earth.

ॐॐ

Your Soul Existence

*Y*our soul is the *perfect* part of you that is
eternal. Your soul existed *before your birth* in
this lifetime, and, your soul will continue to exist
after your physical death. Your soul is your wonderful, totally loving, *true* being that resides in the
spiritual realm, and, *your soul also shares your present
human life with you.*

ৡৡ

Your Soul's Journey

*Y*our soul is involved in *a great cosmic journey through time and space.* On that journey, your soul projects a portion of its Divine Consciousness into human form lifetime after lifetime. This ongoing manifestation of your soul creates *a remarkable sequence of human lives that you* have lived on earth through the ages. *You have passed through the temporary cycles of life and death many times on your way to mastery of the physical world.*

ॐॐ

Your Awareness

*I*f you could view yourself in this moment *without the normal limits of human perception,* you would see that you *now* have within yourself the key to awakening to your eternal nature. That key is your *awareness.* You can *choose* to use that awareness to awaken to the Divine in any moment of your life.

ॐ

Your Desire To Know

*Y*our soul has placed into you a powerful *curiosity*, and a yearning to know more about *all* aspects of life. If you follow that Divine impulse and open your awareness to the eternal realms through a spiritual practice, you can achieve an experience of the spiritual realities that will make your life on earth *richer*, more *joyful*, and more filled with *love*.

৵৶

Returning Home

When you have a desire to consciously know the eternal realities, then you are stirring up a desire to return to *your true existence as a soul—your true home.* However, that is not accomplished by *escaping* earth life. It is done by *completing* your earth adventure with love.

᎒

Your Intuitive Ability

*Y*ou have within you an innate *intuitive ability* to experience the majesty of your soul. By practicing a period of meditation or *attunement* each day, you can open that ability and become aware of a powerful love flowing into you from your soul. The more that you feel that love during your spiritual practice, the more it will manifest in your experience of daily life.

෨෴

A Daily Attunement

*T*hrough a daily spiritual practice, you can expand your inner vision to see more deeply into yourself. In time, you will be able to gaze deeply into *the mysteries of existence.*

༄

Awareness Of The Divine

*A*lthough the loving energies from the Divine realms are continually flowing into you, they do not usually appear to your conscious awareness because humans over time have gradually lost the early clairvoyance that enabled them to directly perceive the Divine realms. Now, for humans to attain conscious awareness of those realms, it must be done through the higher development of *their own inner nature*. This is what you can achieve through a daily spiritual practice.

৩৩৫

You Are An Eternal Soul

*E*vents in the outer world come and go. *You* are permanent. You are presently *a human self* who, after your physical death, will realign with the magnificent Divine reality of *you-as-an-eternal-soul.* If you find yourself struggling with the complexities and challenges of the temporary physical world, you can regain your inspiration by reminding yourself: *"I am an eternal soul. Nothing can damage my being."*

༄

Wisdom From Your Soul

*Y*ou have a spiritual teacher within you. That teacher is *your soul*. If you take some time each day for a spiritual practice of your choosing, you can expand your consciousness and draw upon wisdom from your soul. Answers that you are seeking can reveal themselves to you in the right time, sometimes in surprisingly creative ways.

ॐ

Discovering Your True Existence

*I*n the present realm of *earth* life, you can choose to focus *only* upon this life, and you can achieve much of importance. However, when you choose to add to your life *a curiosity about your existence in other realms,* you begin an exciting, life-long adventure of discovery of your *true* existence *as an eternal soul.*

ॐ

Your Divine Gift

*W*hen you come into your human life, there is *a transference of consciousness* that takes place. Your soul projects a "ray" of its Divine consciousness from the spiritual realm into an *energy structure* in the physical realm. That energy structure becomes your human *self* that you experience as *you* inside your body. Within that *human-self-energy-structure* is your Divine gift of *self-awareness* that enables you to feel: "I am *me*."

&c&

Enlightenment

*A*s a spiritual seeker, you are walking a pathway of spiritual *enlightenment*. As you move along that pathway, you will discover that enlightenment is an ongoing *process*. It is *a gradual introducing of your human self into an experience of spiritual realities over a period of time through a daily spiritual practice.*

యోళు

A Pristine Space

*W*hen you take moments of time to step back from the constant use of your thoughts and feelings in relation to money, health, relationships, protecting against harm—all of the areas that are "forced upon you" by living in the present society—you can enter into a pristine, spiritual "space" that is not overwhelmed by those concerns. In that space of meditation, or attunement, you can ascend to a more refined level of consciousness where you can experience *the perfect eternal nature of your true being*. Done daily, this practice will enable you to bring more peace and harmony into your daily life.

৯৵

Becoming Aware
Of Your Soul

*Y*our conscious awareness of the spiritual reality of your soul will occur *inside you.* Rather than seeing your soul as a *physical form* in the outer world, you will perceive your soul *in your inner experience* as a profound *presence* of love.

ৡৣৡ

Spiritual Awakening

Spiritual awakening usually comes in *gradual increments of understanding,* not in a bolt from the blue that makes you enlightened for the rest of your life. The best way to guide that process of spiritual awakening is to take a period of time each day to step back completely from the distractions of the physical world to give your full attention to *the all-loving Divine Forces of life* that constantly pour into you and sustain you.

৩৵৶

Daily Opportunities

*B*eing impatient to do great things in the world will blind you to the profound importance of your simple *day to day activities*. Being patient, and taking the time to savor the opportunities to touch other people with kindness, compassion, and love day by day will reveal to you *the true magnificence of your gift to humanity*.

৽৹ৎ

Receiving

*W*hen you act to accomplish something in the physical world, you use your *will, strength, determination,* and *forcefulness*—you *pour out* your energies. In your daily spiritual practice, you will be *gentle, receptive,* and *passive*—you will *take in* the loving energies of the Divine.

৯৫

Releasing Your Will

*D*uring your daily spiritual attunement, you can practice putting aside your *will*. By doing that, your inner experience will not be manipulated by you. This opens the way for your experience *to be created by your soul*. Your soul can bring you the experience that is most beneficial and inspiring for you in that moment.

༻◦❀◦༺

Your Inner Goodness

*A*s you move along your spiritual pathway, it will be important for you to feel *the true core of goodness* that exists within your human *self* beneath any negative *experiences* that you might have. That goodness is an eternal *energy of love* that pours into you from your soul. By remembering that inner goodness, you will realize that *your soul is always with you,* even during dark moments.

໙ଈ

Expansiveness

*T*he most powerful feelings to inwardly create in order to expand your consciousness are feelings of *openness* and *love*. And, if you begin by creating feelings of love and appreciation for *yourself,* then the stage is set for creating the feelings of *expansiveness* that are needed as a foundation for a deep spiritual experience.

৩৯৫

Applying Spiritual Teachings

When you are trying to decide which spiritual teachings are best for you to study, or which teacher you want to follow, remember that what is most important is: *How you apply what you learn to your daily life.* Spiritual teachers only show you a *direction.* The *true learning* occurs *within you* as you sincerely *live out* your spiritual ideals day by day.

❧

Your Inner Wisdom

*I*f you do not have a spiritual teacher to guide you on your pathway, trust that you have an ability to access your own *inner source of wisdom.* Through your spiritual practice, and by turning your daily thoughts and feelings toward Divine Love, you can discover that source and draw upon it throughout your life.

৵৵

Appreciating Being Human Again

*A*lthough your soul expresses through many lifetimes on earth, you will have only one life as your *present* human self. Therefore, encourage yourself to feel that each moment of your present life is precious. Fill each moment with gratitude for this truly unique opportunity to be in human form again. Vow to live your present life to the fullest.

☙❧

Making The Divine Real

*T*he spiritual realities of life, and the love of Divine beings, may not seem completely "real" to you at times because you do not ordinarily perceive those non-physical realities. However, you can *make* them real inside you by using your *thoughts* and *feelings* to imagine the perfect Divine beings who love you. As you practice that imagining day after day, it will open your intuitive ability so that you can actually *feel* the reality of those beings as a presence of love within your inner experience.

ॐ

Your Mind

Your mind is not an object located in the brain. It is *a living interaction of extraordinary forces and energies that have evolved from the beginning of human time.* Your mind is a brilliant *light of consciousness* that now lives in you as a powerful tool for mastering life on earth.

৵৹৻

The Power Of Your Mind

*E*very thought that you create exercises *the power of your mind* in one way or another. You are free to use that power to create thoughts of criticism and negativity, which can result in misery. Or, you can use that power to create thoughts that reflect *the true goodness* of your eternal soul. Such inspiring thoughts will help you bring *joy* and *love* into your day to day experience.

∽∾

You And A Teacher

*I*f you choose to follow a spiritual teacher, remember that the key is always *you*. *You* need to assess the teachings that you receive to decide for yourself what serves you best in your spiritual awakening.

ৰ৹৵

Expanding Your Awareness

*B*ecause of the present state of restricted human awareness, you are temporarily caught in a narrow vision of what actually exists in life. At times, it may seem that there are no spiritual realities at all. As you expand your awareness you can go beyond that narrow vision and you can *verify for yourself* the existence of *the extraordinary spiritual realities that sustain life on earth.*

ॐ

A Daily Spiritual Focus

*Y*our normal thoughts about all of the things that you need to do each day in the physical world can so fill your awareness that there is no room left for thoughts about the spiritual realities. That is why a daily spiritual focus is so important. In that focus, you willfully *make* room in your awareness for thoughts of the Divine.

ॐ

Expanded Thoughts

*T*he thoughts that you *consistently* create about life day after day will determine the *quality* of your human experience. If your thoughts are constantly critical or negative, your experience will be unsatisfying. If you choose to *expand* your thoughts with *creativity, idealism,* and *love,* then *your experience can begin to reflect the true vastness and beauty of the Divine Creator.*

ର୍ଚ୍ଚ

Your Self And Your Soul

*A*s you walk your spiritual pathway, it is very important for you to know that there is a profound *loving connection* between your human *self* and the forces of your *soul*. The love that joins you to your soul is powerful, uplifting, and can *never* be diminished or lost.

శ్రీ

A Unique Pathway

*T*he way that you open the door to your deep enlightenment experiences will be determined by *your* particular method of working with your inner patterns of *thinking, feeling, envisioning, choosing, willing, desiring,* and *remembering.* Therefore, you will have a pathway of enlightenment that will always be uniquely *yours.*

෧◌ෳ

Celebrating You

*E*ach day, create a sense of *celebration* of *yourself* as a wonderful human being who is orchestrating your particular expression of *thoughts, emotions,* and *actions* in a beautiful and *important* human manifestation on earth.

ৡৣ

Your Free Will And Your Soul

*T*o help you maintain a meaningful focus on your daily life so that you can *fully* enjoy your human experience and exercise your *free will,* your soul usually stays in *the background of your conscious awareness.* Yet, even though you do not ordinarily have a conscious awareness of your soul, through a daily spiritual practice, you can *expand your awareness* to gain an experience of your soul that can deeply inspire you without overshadowing *your freedom to choose* your life experiences.

ཀ྅ལ

Your Attention And Divine Love

*E*nergies of *Divine Love* are *always* pouring into your human self from God. This occurs *beneath* your conscious awareness. How you come to *consciously perceive* that love grows out of *the personal choices* that you make about what to place your *attention* upon, and what you choose to *think, feel,* and *do,* day by day.

৽৵

Creating Love

*C*hoosing to *create* daily experiences of love for yourself, and for the people in your life, makes manifest the ordinarily invisible forces of Creation. You *become* the Divine Forces of life walking on earth in a tangible way, sharing with others an experience of Divine Love.

৽৵

Personal Growth And Spiritual Experience

*W*hen you consistently bring together *personal growth* and *spiritual experience* in each day, you will have everything that you need to live a more fulfilling life. You will create more *friendship* and *love* with other people, and, you will experience strong feelings of *purpose* and *meaning* in your life.

৵৻৶

Discipline

*I*f the choice of always taking the *easier* path in life becomes a strong habit, you will find it difficult to create the *discipline* necessary for doing a daily spiritual practice. When you are willing to make difficult, but beneficial choices in even the small areas of your life each day, you will develop the discipline necessary to maintain a successful spiritual practice.

৵৹৵

Inner Wisdom

*B*y opening to an awareness of your soul, not only will you bring more *creativity, joy,* and *love* into your life, but, you will also connect to a profound source of *inner wisdom* that can give you answers to the important questions that you have about life.

∽∾

Changes In Meditation

The *depth* of your meditation experience can vary from day to day. One day you can have a very profound experience, and the next day you might feel like nothing meaningful is happening. When you are meditating and you are not feeling spiritual at all, remind yourself that your soul is *always* pouring love into you, even when your meditation experience seems ordinary.

৵৵

The Present Moment

*W*hen you want to become *consciously aware* of your soul and the spiritual dimensions of life, you can focus your attention on your experience *in the present moment,* without your attention wandering to the past or the future. For, *it is in the present moment that your awareness will expand to bring you a wonderful experience of your soul loving you.*

৯০৫

Ordinary Moments

Every moment has within it the possibility of achieving an experience of heightened awareness. You can create inspiring experiences of purpose and meaning even in an ordinary, mundane moment in life. This is one of the great spiritual truths.

❦

Your Intuition

*T*he practice of opening your *intuition* is important in the process of your spiritual awakening because your soul and the Divine beings have *non*-physical forms that are not perceived through your physical senses. They need to be *sensed* through your *intuition*.

৩৫

Intuition And Emotion

You can become aware of your soul and the Divine realms through inner experiences of *intuition*. Your intuition is intimately woven with your *emotions*. Therefore, if you practice opening yourself emotionally, you will stimulate the opening of your intuition, making it possible to *sense* and *feel* the loving influence of your soul in your life.

ೂ

Intuition And Divine Energies

*Y*our intuition is the "conduit" through which the Divine Forces of your soul flow into your human self. Your intuition makes those Divine energies available to your *conscious awareness* so that your thoughts and feelings can become inspired beyond your ordinary human experience.

ço&

Emotional Expansion

*E*xpanding your *emotional sensitivity* will stimu-late your ability to *intuitively sense* the Divine realities. The best way to do that is *to extend yourself and to pay more attention to the people in your life.* Through sincere, honest, loving communication with other people, and your willingness to *find the good in them,* you accelerate the expansion of your emotional life, thereby quickening your intuitive abilities.

୨୦୯

Intuition And Criticism

*I*ntuition is a natural ability available within everyone. When you choose to *criticize* yourself and other people, you create an inner tightness of negativity that temporarily blocks your access to that intuitive ability. By transforming your criticisms through understanding, patience, and love, you release that tightness and you open the way to releasing your natural intuitive ability.

৵৶

Feelings Of Goodness

When you create feelings of *goodness about yourself,* and you expand your feelings of goodness *about others,* you have a powerful way to experience life in a deep and meaningful manner. This will stimulate your innate ability to experience *Divine Love.*

෨෬

Self-Preoccupation

*W*hen you choose *to give of yourself to other people,* you transcend the ordinary *self-preoccupation* that envelops all human beings. Through that giving to others, you stimulate an emotional opening within you that becomes a bridge between *yourself,* as you live within your *private reality,* and all that exists *outside* of your subjective experience.

 споу

Your Soul Awareness

*I*n the spiritual realm, *your soul* always has a full awareness of the ongoing eternal experience of *goodness* and *perfect love*. As a *human*, you are the "child" of your soul, and you are learning to *create* that awareness of Divine Love through the expression of your own idealistic thoughts, feelings, and intuitions in your human experience.

৶৶

Receptivity

*A*s you work to achieve what you desire in the *outer* world, you focus on *acting, doing,* and *pouring out* energy to manipulate *physical* realities. In your spiritual practice in your *inner* life, you will be engaging *non*-physical realities. You will need to *take in* and *receive* energy and love. Therefore, in your spiritual practice moments, *receptivity* is more important than strong, willful *action.*

৯৫

Feeling God

*A*chieving a true experience of God is not brought forth simply by *thinking* about God. Although your thoughts and ideas about what God is can be a starting point in your quest, you can learn to go beyond thinking about God by practicing *feeling* God flowing into you as *Divine Love.*

❧

Persistence

One of the most important factors in your spiritual pathway is *persistence*. This means persistence in creating a spiritual focus in your thoughts and feelings each day. When you do that day by day, you will discover *an inner pathway that leads to the higher knowledge that you are seeking.*

కఎ

Sensing Beyond The Physical

*H*uman conscious awareness of the Divine realities has become lost to many through the ages due to *narrow thoughts and beliefs,* and, *an intense focus on physical realities.* By entertaining new and expansive ideas about life, combined with an attunement practice that stimulates your ability to sense beyond physical reality, you can regain the memory of ancient knowledge that you have gained through many lifetimes on earth.

৩৩

Feeling Divine Love

*W*hen you are meditating and you are not *seeing* your soul or God in your inner vision, know that *feeling the Divine Love flowing into you* from your soul or God is more beneficial than an inner vision. Even if your inner vision is blank or empty when you meditate, you can continue to create an inner receptivity and perceive your soul or God through your *intuitive feelings*.

෪

Caring For Others

*D*irecting your *attention,* and your *feelings of caring* toward others will lift you out of limited, self-focused thoughts and feelings. You will become more sensitive to other people, thus creating greater depth in your relationships. Deep, loving relationships *are a catalyst for your personal spiritual awakening.*

৽৵

Your Interactions With Others

*Y*ou can create beautiful experiences for yourself when you slow down in your rush through your daily activities and take more time to pay attention to the people that you interact with. By extending your warmth toward others, and by feeling the goodness of their being, you can begin to discover eternal connections that you have with the people in your life. You can come to understand that *there are important soul purposes in each interaction that you have with those people.*

ༀ

New States Of Consciousness

*W*hen you pay attention to other people, and you open your heart to feel them deeply, care for them, and love them, you are also, without noticing it, opening yourself to spiritual energies from your soul and from God. That stimulates *new states of consciousness in which your awareness can go beyond your ordinary experience in the physical world.*

৩৵৵

Opportunity And Choices

*T*oday is your day of *opportunity*. You have the opportunity to make choices in kindness and love, which will move your life in the direction of *mastery of earth life*. Remind yourself that you *create* your life day by day *through the choices that you make.*

৵৵

The Voice Of God

*W*hen you speak words of kindness, compassion, and love, *you become the voice of God on earth.*

ೢംಎ

A Perfect World

*A*s you start your day today, imagine that you are going out into a *perfect* world. Imagine how you would like other people in that perfect world to treat you. What would be the perfect way that they would behave toward you? Then, as you go about your day, *treat other people in just that perfect way.* If you do that, you will be doing your part in the creation of a perfect world.

৽৵

The Illusion Of Distance

*T*he primary need during a silent attunement is *to feel that you are loved by Divine beings.* That experience will dissolve the temporary illusion of *distance* between your human self, your soul, your guiding souls, and God. For, in truth, *there is no distance.* The Divine beings are *never* distant from your human self.

৯৹৵

Intensity

O ne of the reasons that souls choose to manifest on earth is to gain experiences of *intensity*.
Thus, there is an innate "craving" in humans for
intense experience. When that craving is turned
toward the pursuit of sensual pleasure in the negative sense, it can become an "addiction." By turning
that craving toward the pursuit of *uplifting* experiences of intensity, such as companionship,
intimacy, love, and spiritual experience, you will be
fulfilling your soul's intention of gaining intense
human experience in the most *masterful* way.

ৡৄৢ

Managing Negative Feelings

At times, you can feel trapped in feelings of sadness, despair, fear, and other negative emotions. This is an opportunity to *manage* those feelings in a loving, confident, creative way. Negative feelings can actually become a step, rather than a stumbling block, on your path to higher consciousness. You take that step by entering the feelings briefly, then releasing them and reminding yourself: "The negativity is *temporary. I am an eternal soul. These negative feelings cannot damage my being.*"

❧

Kindness

*E*very day, do at least one kind thing for yourself, and one kind thing for someone else. Even something as simple as a kind word, a gesture, a touch, or an embrace is an important contribution to the unfoldment of Divine Goodness on earth.

ço﹏﹏

Your Attitude
Toward Yourself

A powerful way to deepen your meditation experience is to make creative adjustments in *the attitude that you take toward yourself as a person.* The way that you see yourself, and the feelings that you create about yourself, will have a powerful impact upon what you experience when you meditate. If you take the attitude that there is a wonderful spiritual center of goodness within you that can never be lost, then you can create a solid foundation for achieving a deep spiritual experience during your meditation.

෨ᵔᏬ

Negativity And Your True Goodness

*W*ith any negative thoughts and feelings that you might create about yourself, you can train yourself to accept them as *temporary human experiences*, not as *truths* about who you are as a being. With a *spiritual* vision, you can look *through* the negativity and see *the true goodness* of yourself beneath it all.

৩৵৶

Meditation And Expectations

*Y*our meditation experiences will be *unique to you*. If you release your expectations about what those experiences *should* be, you open the way for allowing the experiences to be what they *need to be* for your greatest benefit.

ை

Giving To Yourself

*T*oday, practice giving to *yourself* the same kindness and respect that you would give to a person that you deeply love.

৯৽৶

Daily Life

*W*hen you practice perceiving the Divine presence of God in your daily life, then even the most mundane moments of an ordinary experience can become exhilarating.

৩৯৫

Loving Yourself

*Y*our human *self* has within it all of the attributes of the Divine. By learning to heal your self-criticism, and by *your willingness to love your human self,* you can directly experience the Divine *within you.*

৯৹৶

The Human
And The Divine

As you practice each day feeling the love flowing into yourself from the Divine, and then you *act* in ways that express that love to the people around you, *you are fulfilling a great purpose for which you came into earth as a human being in this lifetime.* That purpose is: *To merge the human and the Divine on earth.*

❧❦

Mastery Through Sharing

*C*hoosing to share yourself with others through a smile, or a simple kind word, is *the willful expansion of spiritual energies coming through you to another person.* If you extend that throughout your lifetime, then you will achieve a great *personal* mastery, and, you will make a magnificent contribution to life on earth.

ॐ

Points Of Consciousness

*Y*ou live *within Universal Consciousness.* Your earth life is *one* of your points of consciousness. As a *soul,* you have many different points of consciousness, including the human, and they are *all* infused with the perfect love of the Divine.

৵৶

A Life Of Love

*B*y your willingness to continually *choose* to live a life of *love,* you are living the life that was intended for humans to create on earth. By living that life, you become *a conscious co-creator* with the Divine.

ༀ

Rejuvenation

*Y*our *meditation experiences*, your *thoughts about your spiritual ideals*, and, *seeing your goodness as God sees it*, all send rejuvenating signals to every cell in your body, inviting an increase of health throughout the body.

ॐ

Awareness And Pure Love

*D*uring your meditation, it is very important to remember that *the fluctuation of your awareness*—from ordinary awareness to an awareness of the Divine—is only a fluctuation of *your human consciousness.* The Divine Forces of love *never* fluctuate. They never withdraw from your human self. That pure love *always pours forth into you without ceasing.*

༺࿇༻

Ordinary And Spiritual Experience

Spiritual experience is not the *opposite* of ordinary human experience. Indeed, it is an *expanded version* of the ordinary, just as the ocean is an expanded version of a puddle in which you stand.

⋙⋘

Your Spiritual Life

*I*f you understand that you are an eternal *soul,* then even when you are having an experience in which you say, "This is not a spiritual moment," you would know that indeed it *is* spiritual, because *you* are having it, and you are spiritual. You are an eternal soul, *a spiritual being,* and, therefore, every moment you live is a spiritual moment.

৵৵

You And A Future Lifetime

You are the one who will decide if you will return to earth for another lifetime in the future. You will never be forced to return to earth life as a punishment. *You-as-a-soul* will know if you left anything untouched by love, and you can choose to return to earth to complete what was left undone.

❧

Trust

On your spiritual pathway, one of the most important feelings to cultivate is the feeling of *trust*. You will learn to trust that Divine beings are *continually* loving you even when you have no sense of their presence. Therefore, you can *trust* that you are never alone.

৵৵

Negativity And Goodness

*A*ll human negativity is *temporary*. The *goodness* of God is the *permanent* reality that sustains human life on earth. The entire fabric of the cosmos is woven with that *eternal* goodness.

 educ

Your Vision Of Yourself

*Y*our spiritual practice can expand your vision of *yourself as a person.* Instead of being restricted to the *ordinary* human viewpoint that can at times show you limit and lack in yourself, you can learn to see yourself with *an enlightened vision* that will reveal the wonderful inner *goodness* that lives within you.

ভ∞ঞ

The Outside World
And Your Inner Life

*T*he outside world cannot force thoughts and feelings upon you. You *create* your thoughts and feelings in your inner life *in response* to the events of the outer world. Regardless of what happens in the outside physical world, *you always have the inner power to create the thoughts, feelings, and attitudes that most benefit you in your life.*

༄༅

Your Guiding Souls

*I*n periods of *harmony* and *peace* in your life, if you build a strong belief in the *majesty* and *perfect love* of the Divine souls who guide you, then, when you are struggling with a challenge, you will more easily feel the energies of strength, wisdom, and love that are pouring into you from those eternal beings.

౨∾౿

Hearing Your Guides

*T*here are many ways in which the souls who guide you—but who do not take human voice—speak to you *in the gentle inner recesses of your own human awareness.* Those beings will nudge you to go forth in your life toward individuals and circumstances that will *stimulate* you, *inspire* you, and *uplift* you in creative, beneficial ways.

ೞൿ

Your Hunger To Fulfill

*Y*our soul has placed into your human *self* a deep hunger to merge with other human beings in love, and a hunger to know the eternal while in human form. The reason that your soul has given you that hunger is to move you toward an important purpose of your human life on earth, which is: *To merge the human with the Divine, and to manifest that divinity in your relationships with other people.*

❧

The Center Of The Universe

*Y*our present human *self*, in terms of *your inner experience*, exists at the center of the universe. From that center point, *your inner experience has no limit.* You can *imagine* outward in all directions into infinity.

৯৽

Releasing Burdens

*B*y practicing the release of your burdens of regret, disappointment, self-doubt, and guilt, you peel back layers of confusion to open the way to a direct experience of the *Divine Goodness* that has been placed into you by your soul.

༄༃

Co-Creating With God

*Y*ou become a *co-creator* with God when you consistently choose to express *kindness, compassion,* and *love* to others in your daily life. Through such *choices,* you create a powerful goodness in the human world *that extends the magnificence of the Divine into the physical realm.*

࿐

Higher Consciousness

*E*xperiences of *higher consciousness* are achieved by the way that you live, and by *the way that you create your daily thoughts.* Therefore, using your powerful mind to create uplifting thoughts in each day is an important step on your path to higher consciousness.

ু৯৫

Your Purpose In Life

*I*f you are wondering what your purpose in life might be, know that if you do nothing else except love other people and yourself while you are in human form, then you will fulfill one of your most important purposes as a human being. You will be moving toward the splendid completion of your earth journey.

ৎৡ

The Essence Of God

*Y*our experience of God depends upon the *feelings* that you bring forth within yourself about the *essence* of God, and not upon a visible *form* that you attribute to God. In other words, you will need to *feel* whatever God *is*, rather than trying to *see* what God *looks like*.

ৡ৶

Selfishness And Generosity

*T*he underlying cause of human negativity is *selfishness.* When you act out of selfishness you are contributing to that negativity. When you act out of generosity and sensitivity to others, then you join *the force of good* that is helping to heal negativity on earth.

ॐ

Demonstrating Love

*I*f you *fully* use your ability to care about others, and to be kind to them, you will be making *real* a great truth of life, which is: *All humans are joined by an unending Divine Love.* However, for humans to become *consciously aware* of that love, it is not enough to simply feel it inside yourself. It needs to be *demonstrated* through your daily actions with others in the world.

෨෴

Choosing Your Thoughts

You build your life daily by the *thoughts* that you choose and carry forward as *habits*. So, today, remember how powerful your thoughts are, and remind yourself that you can *choose ones that inspire you and help you feel the true goodness of life.*

ৎৡ

Enlightenment As A Goal

*T*o achieve experiences of enlightenment, you will need to make that goal as important to you as your goals in the physical world.

ॐ

Teachings Of The Masters

*T*he true teachings of the *Spiritual Masters* of the present and the past are centered in *kindness, compassion,* and *love.* The closer you can come to living kindness, compassion, and love each day, the more *you will fulfill your purposes in life,* and, the more *you will bless others* by living the true teachings of the Masters in your interactions with the people in your life.

ﻌﻌ

Aloneness

*F*eelings of *aloneness* and *isolation* are *temporary self-creations* that can be transformed by awakening to the Divine Love that constantly pours into you from God. The *final* healing of feelings of aloneness will come when you awaken to the spiritual bonds of love that tie you to others, and you take that love forward to share it with other people in your world.

༝

Time And Timelessness

*T*he counting of *time* is simply a convenient human enterprise. Your *being* is *timeless* —it is eternal.

∽∾

Your Soul's Experience

I n addition to loving you and sustaining you in the *human* realm, at the same time your soul is having a vast, unlimited creative experience that is shared with all other souls in the *spiritual* realm, and with the Divine Forces of life that are God.

ৡৰ

Your Soul's Place

*D*uring your daily spiritual practice, in order to remember that *you are your soul*, it can be helpful to simply think of your soul as a very real and wonderful "place" of *perfect loving experience* inside you. When you go to that place, whether during meditation, or in a silent moment during the day, *you will feel as if you have come home.*

ৡৎ

Gifts From Your Soul

*Y*ou can think of your soul as *a vast reservoir of wisdom, courage, strength, creativity, comfort, love,* and even wise *answers* to your questions about life. That reservoir exists *inside you,* and, through your spiritual practice, you can learn to tap in to it so that you can draw upon those beneficial gifts from your soul.

ঔৎ৶

Loving Yourself

*L*oving yourself is important in preparing your emotions for an opening to the Divine. You will be able to love yourself more fully if you are willing to view yourself as *a fascinating, multifaceted being with many admirable qualities and talents that you are in the process of uncovering and expressing in your daily life.* That can help you awaken to the truth that *you are indeed a remarkable being who has been sent into earth life by your soul for very important purposes.*

ℰℴℰ

Significant Relationships

*A*s you pay more attention to the people in your life, and as you try to express your sensitivity and kindness to them, then your daily interactions with others that you might have previously considered to be mundane and ordinary will take on a deeper *significance*. You can begin to discover important *soul purposes* that you are playing out in those relationships. You can begin to experience profound levels of *meaningfulness* and *love* in your connections with other people.

ৎৡৡ

Persistence And Focus

I f your goal is to awaken spiritually, then you can achieve that goal through *persistence in doing your daily spiritual practice,* combined with *persistence in taking a spiritual viewpoint as you carry out your daily activities in the world.*

ভৈ

Spiritual Expectations

$\mathcal{B}$e flexible with your *expectations* about the spiritual experiences that you are seeking. If you can only find significance in *one* kind of spiritual experience that you *prefer*, then you are limiting yourself. When you can find purpose and meaning *in the entire range* of experiences that you have in your spiritual practice, from the ordinary to the deeply inspiring, then you will be truly *mastering* the process of spiritual awakening.

ๆๆ

Inner Peace

*E*ven in the chaos of human life in the outer physical world, you can create a refreshing moment of *inner peace*. Simply focus on your breath and experience with all of your senses the perfect love that is woven into the Divine silence.

ॐ

A Full Expression Of You

When you live each day *merging the human and the Divine* by bringing together *your personal growth* and *your spiritual experiences,* you are choosing to move toward a *full* expression of yourself in ways that will *complete the important purposes that your soul has given you in this lifetime.*

ৡৣ

The Quality Of Your Future

*T*oday, remind yourself that the *quality* of your choices, your *thoughts*, and your *feelings* in the *present* day will determine the quality of your life experience in *future days*. You create your life's path by the important choices that you make *today*.

ജ്ഞരു

Wielding The Power Of Your Will

*T*he power of your *will* has been given to you by God. You exercise that power through the *choices* that you make in your life day by day. When your choices reflect your *ideals,* then you are wielding the power of your will in the beneficial way that was *intended.*

৩৵

Your Part In Creation

When you gaze at the sky at night, contemplate the thought that *you-as-a-soul* played a part, with other souls, in wielding the forces of God to create the physical universe. Imagine the majesty of your soul and its infinite movement within all of Creation.

෧ල

Choosing Love

*E*ven though the fabric of the universe is infused with Divine Love, that love will not *force* you personally toward goodness. You must *choose* to create experiences in life that *mirror* that Divine Love, then *the goodness will manifest through you.*

৵৹৻

Experiences Of Intensity

*A*n important purpose for coming to earth over many lifetimes is to give your soul certain experiences of *intensity* that can be gained in the *physical* reality. That is why *every* experience in your life is significant in your personal evolution through life on earth.

❧

Healing Negativity

*A*s you gain in wisdom, you will see more and more clearly that human motives rooted in *selfishness* lie at the heart of challenges between people. You will also come to know with certainty that if your motives are based in a desire to *understand* and *help* other people, then *you become a strong force for the healing of negativity on earth.*

୬∞෬

Creating Love For Yourself

*A*s you prepare to begin your day, you can create a beginning of inspiration by saying to yourself: "In all of the complex threads of human experience that I will weave together and manage in this day, I promise to create some moments of *love and appreciation for myself.*"

ॐ

Spiritual Qualities

*T*wo very important *spiritual qualities* that you have within your human self are the limitless power of *mind*, and the majesty of your infinite imagination. *These are human reflections of the Divine qualities of the Creator of life.*

৽৹৶

Trusting Your Inner Goodness

*T*o *fully* awaken to the Divine Spirit that lives within you, it will be important to continually acknowledge *the human goodness* of you as a person. Even if your daily choices and actions are not always perfect, you can *trust* that *beneath* those choices and actions, *there is a human goodness that is linked to the perfect Divine Spirit within you.*

ॐ

Deeper Meanings

*T*o understand *the mystery of your true relation-ship to the Divine Forces,* you must penetrate the *surface* of life as it is presented to you in the physical world. You will look for *deeper meanings* in your daily experiences, and in your relationships with the people in your life. Those deeper mean-ings can be *intuitively sensed* if you will practice opening your intuition through a daily spiritual practice over a period of time. You will discover how your experiences and your relationships with others *are always connected to the overall purposes of the Divine Forces.*

৵৹

The People In Your Life

*I*n your willingness to practice *patience* with the people in your life, there comes an *expansion of your consciousness* that allows you to go beyond your own limited perceptions of those people. Being patient with others will open the way for you *to awaken to a deeper truth about who those people really are, and why they are in your life.*

༄

People Who Challenge You

*I*t is easy to love the people in your life who please you. When you have the courage to have compassion for those who challenge you, then *you become a more potent emissary of God on earth.*

৯৫

Your Experiences
And Your Soul

*I*n your soul, there are no *contradictions*. There are no *opposites*. *All* of your human experiences are *important* to your soul, whether you consider them to be positive experiences or negative experiences.

॰॰॰

Individuality And Unity

*A*s a *soul,* you have an ongoing experience of unity with the all-loving Divine Forces of God. As a *human,* you have the very intense experience of *individuality.* Through your spiritual awakening, you can gain an awareness of *the soul experience of unity.* Then, you can integrate that with *your human experience of individuality.* By doing that, you will create *a mastery of life on earth.*

ॐ

Aspects Of Creation

*A*s a human, you are playing your part in the eternal process of *coming to know Creation in all of its aspects.* You gain that knowledge when your *individual* consciousness aligns with the *unity* consciousness of the Divine Creator. Then, *you will experience yourself as part of every soul, and, as part of everything that exists.*

৽৽

Your Cosmic Adventure

*T*o live a meaningful and fulfilling human life, you do not need to be *consciously aware* of the other worlds and dimensions of existence that you are part of as a soul. But, by *thinking* about those hidden realities as part of the vastness of your being, *you can feel that you have important purposes in your human life that are part of a cosmic adventure through the vastness of existence.*

৵৻

Cosmic Secrets

*T*here are *cosmic secrets* buried deep within your human consciousness which you ordinarily cannot reach. Through your daily spiritual attunements, you will be able to penetrate to those deeper levels, bring those secrets into the light of your conscious awareness, and truly understand yourself as a *complete* being.

୭∾ଏ

The Physical
And The Spiritual

*H*umans have been "conditioned" to believe only what they can see, and touch, and *prove* in the *physical* sense. However, if you limit your experience of life to that, you will gradually lose touch with the *spiritual realities* which *cannot* be seen, touched, and proven in the physical sense. Through a daily spiritual practice, you can learn to directly *experience* within you, the majesty of the eternal realms that cannot be perceived in the outer world.

ॐ

The Power Of Your Will

*A*s a human, you are now, in the *largest* sense, the result of what you have done with your *free will* through many lifetimes. If you do not like that result, the key is to *change the way that you use your free will.* Using your will in *kindness, compassion,* and *love* will result in the fulfilling life that you desire.

༄

Creating Kindness

*E*veryone can agree that there is a need for kindness and love in the world, but who will bring that forward on a daily basis? Will it be *you*?

∽❧

Returning To Your Source

*I*f you understand that in your cosmic journey *you are on the way back to your source,* then you will come to realize that *your present human life is a very important step on that journey.* The more that you can live this life in goodness and love, the more magnificent will be the gifts that you bring back to your Creator in the end.

಄

The Mystery Of Death

*B*y connecting with your soul, you can solve the great mystery of *death*. You will be able to remember that *you* do not die when your physical body dies. You will remember that *you have a magnificent ongoing spiritual existence that continues beyond death.*

જ્જ

The Doorway Of Death

You have passed through the doorway of death many times. After each lifetime there is a celebration of your life. To help you remember, you can envision the souls who love you welcoming you with great exuberance and joy—rejoicing in your return home.

᠙᠊ᢀ

Your Awareness After Death

W hat you experience as *you-as-a-human* is a small portion of the larger awareness of *you-as-an-eternal-soul*. The rest of your soul awareness is temporarily hidden from your human self awareness while you are alive. When your body dies, that 'ray' of soul consciousness that has been your experience of your human self is returned to the *full* soul awareness in the eternal realm. Then, what you have been experiencing as *you* simply stops being small, and it becomes extraordinarily large. *Your human self wakes up to its full existence as a magnificent eternal soul.*

જ્જ

Pleasure And Ease

*T*hings that bring you pleasure and ease in your physical life will not block your spiritual unfoldment unless you make them your highest ideal and you use them selfishly.

ೲಎ

Building In Consciousness

*W*hen you pass through the door of death, your human attainments of *consciousness* from your present lifetime will be added to what you have accomplished in your many past lifetimes on earth. Therefore, it is wise to ask yourself: "*What am I building in consciousness in this lifetime that will be added to my soul?*"

৽৹

Healing Emotional Pain

*A*ll over the world, there are people who are struggling with *emotional pain.* Your willingness to extend *kindness* to the people that you encounter each day may seem like a small gesture in light of the overall suffering in the world. However, *your daily expression of kindness* actually has a "ripple" effect that becomes *an important contribution to the healing of emotional pain worldwide.*

✌∾❧

Your Path Of Mastery

*E*ach experience that you have in each day is a step on the important pathway of *mastery* that you are walking in human life on earth. Some of those steps can be painful, some are easy and joyful. The important thing is not to lose sight of the *progress* that you have made on your path, and to know that the challenges are *temporary,* while your inner ability to master those challenges is *permanent.* That is an ability given to you by the all-loving Divine Forces of God.

৵৹৶

Choosing And Mastery

*T*here are many ways to live a human life, and you have the freedom to *choose* your own way. If you become confused about what is the *best* way to live in order to *master* life on earth, always know that choosing to live a life of *idealism,* based on *kindness, compassion,* and *love,* along with *a willingness to sincerely seek an awareness of Divine Love,* will bring the most fulfillment and mastery possible for a human being.

৵৵

The Eternal You

*T*he challenges of your life last only for a while.
You last for eternity.

ༀ

The Mystery Of Your Life

*Y*our life as a human is *a profound mystery.* You cannot *see* where you came from before your birth, nor can you *see* where you will go after your death. However, you can learn to *intuitively sense* the reality of your Divine beginning, and your ongoing expression in the perfect *Eternal Now* that extends beyond the door of death.

༺◦༻

Your Inner Purity

*T*he purity of an innocent child shines forth *naturally* for all to see. It is a Divine quality within the child. That same purity lives within *you* as an adult. How much it shines out to others will be determined by how *open* and *loving* you are in your relationships with the people around you.

ৼ৹৵

True Greatness

*T*he *truly great individual* is not the one who stands large in terms of fame or wealth in the world. It is the one who has *the spirit of love,* and *the courage to share that love with people in the world through action.*

৯৽৵

Desire

*D*esire is a *power* that drives you to act and achieve in the world. When your desires are acted upon with kindness and sensitivity to the needs of others, *you attract allies to help you fulfill those desires.*

৩৩

Thoughts As A Bridge

*P*hysical forces manifest only in the *material* plane of existence. Your *mental energies* manifest both in the physical plane as your conscious thoughts, and, *in the spiritual dimensions* as invisible energies. Therefore, *your thoughts can be a bridge between the human and the Divine.*

৽৵

Using Your Memory

*W*hen you use your *memory*, you are free to focus upon impressions of the past that you consider to be negative. You can recall those negative memories in the present and convince yourself that you can never be happy because you have been hurt by pain in the past. You are also free to remind yourself that the past is *ended*, and, that *memories cannot damage your being.* Then, *you are free to release the negative memories,* and, *you are free to create new inspiring thoughts and feelings in the present.*

৯৹ৎ

Positive Thoughts

*T*he more that you consistently use your mind to create positive thoughts, images, and ideas, *the easier it is for your soul to nudge your mind toward what benefits you the most in your life.*

৵৵

Challenge And Fulfillment

*B*less *every* experience that you have as an important step in your mastery of life on earth. Even challenging experiences can be seen as stepping stones that *stimulate your courage, strength, and wisdom,* taking you one step closer to personal fulfillment in your life.

୨୦୧

The Divine Forces And Health

The Divine Forces of God are the all-powerful *life-sustaining* energies that quicken every cell of your physical body. They sustain the energy structure that you experience as your human *self*. When you can feel this, then you can begin to *consciously align your thoughts and feelings with the perfect love of those Divine Forces,* not only for experiences of joy and fulfillment for your human self, but also *for the ongoing stimulation of strength and health in your physical body.*

Sharing Love

*T*o retreat into a daily spiritual practice can be very beneficial for *you*. However, the *full* awakening to *Divine Love* comes when you go out into the world *to share your love with the people around you.*

৯৫

Consistency

*C*reative manifestation through the power of your *mind* is not done by one *single* thought. It is done by *consistent thinking, consistent imaging,* and *consistent action* in the world.

৵৶

Your Being And Creation

*Y*our *body* will die in the physical plane, but your *being* will not, for your being is a magnificent thread of the tapestry of *eternal life*. You are exquisitely *unique*, and, you are part of the beauty of the *whole* of Creation.

ൟൟ

Your Spiritual Awakening

*Y*ou, and the people around you, are fellow travelers on the road to *a full spiritual awakening.* When you help them along on their pathway through your *kindness* and *love,* you move swiftly and gracefully toward *your own awakening.*

ᕦᐧᕤ

The Hope For Humanity

*I*f you become discouraged about negativity in the world, know that those humans who commit themselves to *kindness, compassion,* and *love,* and then try to integrate that into their words and behaviors, *are the hope for humanity.* The souls will not force humans to stop being frightened and stop creating negativity. It requires *humans* to touch the confused ones who are creating negativity, and that is done through the expression of *compassion* and *understanding.* That will eventually help the confused ones to *heal their fears.*

෧෧

Your Expression
Of The Divine

*L*ife is *a spiritual force,* and it is *continuous.* It manifests in different planes of consciousness. It is *presently* manifesting in *you* as a wonderful human *self* inhabiting your physical body on earth. As you awaken to that truth, and as you honor your present human self as an important expression of the Divine, *you open the way for great fulfillment and completion in this lifetime.*

ക്ക

Imagination And Divine Beings

*U*sing the wings of your *imagination,* you can fly to every corner of the universe. By doing that with a profound *love,* you will discover *everywhere* the presence and the perfect companionship of the Divine beings who love you throughout your existence.

☙☙

Beneficial Human Qualities

*A*mong the many beneficial human qualities that you can choose to cultivate—and there are many important ones—of great significance are *perseverance, patience,* and *trust.* If you add those to *kindness, compassion,* and *love,* you will live a most fulfilling life.

ॐ

Your Perception
Of The Divine

*Y*our human perception of the Divine is always at a temporary stage. Even as you achieve a deeper experience of the spiritual realms, *celebrate what you gain,* but, remind yourself that *there is always more that you will discover as you walk your spiritual pathway.*

ക്കൈ

The Kingdom Of God

*I*f *all* humans could *perfectly* manifest kindness and love in daily life, there would be no doubt that there is a God. You would feel, "I *know* that I live in the kingdom of God because every human that I meet is perfectly kind to me, and loves me in a *God-like* way, and *I love every human that I meet in the same way.*"

℔ℕ

Spiritual Beauty

*W*hen you create *physical* beauty in the human world, you are directly reflecting the *spiritual* beauty of the Divine.

৯৵

Understanding Divine Love

*W*ith the complexity of human *thought* and *language* that exists at the present time, it can be difficult to find a clear *definition* of Divine Love in *words*. But, in your spiritual practice, you can learn to *feel* that love in a way that goes far beyond words.

৵৵

The Language Of Your Soul

*Y*our spiritual practice can help you learn the "language" of your soul. The language of your soul is not a language of *words*. It is an extraordinary *experience* that could be called, *harmony, beauty, goodness,* and *love* in its most *intense* form.

ৡৰ

From The Ordinary
To The Extraordinary

A spiritual practice has great benefit because it enables you to step back from your familiar thoughts, feelings, and repetitive human experiences that you have become used to in your life. This frees you from the *ordinary*, opening you to the *extraordinary*, as new powerful and inspiring thoughts and feelings are stimulated in your awareness by your soul.

∽∾

Receiving And Trusting

*Y*our spiritual practice allows you to put aside the part of your human self that believes, "I must *push* and *force* life toward goodness, or goodness will not occur." As you do that, you will be able to create the *receptive, trusting* feelings that are needed in order to become aware of Divine Love flowing into you.

৩৵৶

Awakening To The Divine In Others

A powerful way to awaken to the Divine Forces that live within every person that you meet is to remind yourself: "This person now standing in front of me is *an eternal soul* who has come through time and space, just as I have, to arrive at this present moment that we are sharing."

৯৽৶

Doubt About The Divine

*I*n your spiritual practice, if you have not yet had a profound experience of the Divine, you can have doubts about that reality. In that case, it is a matter of patiently *training* yourself to *believe*, and *trust*, that there *are* beloved souls, that there *is* the Divine Love, that there *is* God. Then, by practicing opening your heart in love, you can have an experience that dispels all doubt about the *reality* of Spirit. You can truly *experience* Divine Love pouring into you. In that moment, you will know for certain that the Divine Love emanates from God, and you will know that you are *always* loved by God.

৵৶

Spiritual Guidance

*I*f you seek *spiritual guidance* during your attunement, at times you can sense a strong "urging" that seems to be more than your usual conscious thinking and feeling. This can be an intuitive nudging from your soul to help you move toward choices in life that serve you best. This nudging would not be so strong that it would overwhelm your freedom to *choose*, but, *it would predispose you to make a wiser choice.*

૭∼ન્ડ

Condemning And Forgiving

*E*ach time that you *condemn* yourself, or you condemn another person, you add intensity to the patterns of confusion in your thoughts that prevent you from penetrating to the inner *goodness* of yourself or the other person. Each time that you *forgive* and *love*, you free yourself from such limitation.

୭৵

Suffering And The Miracle Of You

*I*f you have suffered quite a bit in your life, you might conclude that life is *bad*, that there can never be ongoing joy, goodness, or love. Those are understandable *thoughts* and *feelings*. However, they are *temporary*. They do not change the underlying *truth*, which is: Human life on earth is an extraordinary *miracle*. It is a miracle that *eternal souls*, wielding the forces of God *outside of time and space*, have managed to create marvelous human bodies on earth into which they project a ray of *Divine Consciousness* as a human *self*. As you see this, you can understand that it is a *miracle* that you are *you* in this moment of time.

ৡৡ

Kindness And Healing

*T*oday, think about, and look for, "kindness opportunities." Think to yourself: *"Every person that I interact with today brings me an opportunity to practice kindness."* If you are willing to seize that opportunity and act upon it, you will be doing your part in healing human negativity on earth.

࿐

Feelings Of Badness

You can keep learning that any feelings of *badness* that you might have at any time are *temporary*. The *goodness* within your human self is *eternal*. If you can remember that, then you will thrive throughout this lifetime.

∽◦∾

The Power Of Your Attitude

*Y*our human life brings you many different kinds of experiences. Whether those experiences are painful or joyful for you depends in part on people and events in the outside world. However, *within* you is the power to adjust your *attitude* toward those people and events so that you can discover that there is some kind of *benefit* in any experience, positive or negative.

৵৹৵

A Perfect Love

The perfect Divine beings who love you are constantly pouring into you a love that *has no limit*. It is a love that does not demand, nor criticize. It is a love that is *full*, and *complete*, and *pure*, and *wonderful*. It is a love that is *always* given to you, *no matter what you do in your life*.

৵৹৹

Spiritual Teachings

*R*emember that *spiritual teachings are created by humans*. They are *words* that are passed along in spoken or written form. Through your spiritual awakening, you can *experience truth for yourself* in a way that goes *beyond* words.

༄༅

Your Talents And Mastery

*E*ach day, let yourself feel how *important* it is that you are living as a human being on earth right now. As you live out each day, know that *you are expressing talents and abilities that have been placed into your human self by your soul for very important purposes.* Though it may take time to become aware of those talents, your process of *discovering* them and *using* them in the world can be an exciting aspect of your *mastery* of life on earth.

୭∽୧

Universal Oneness

All reality, in all realms, and in all dimensions, is part of the grand tapestry of *Universal Oneness* that unites all beings. Therefore, there is no *separation* in any dimension of reality.

৯৵

Regrets About Relationships

*E*very day, ask yourself: "If I were to die today, would I have any regrets about my relationships with the people in my life?" If so, *now* is the time to do something about it if you can.

❧

Your Unique Vision Of God

*T*oday, hold this thought in your mind: "One of my purposes in this lifetime, in addition to the attainment of the goals and ideals that I set for myself, is to create *my own unique, individual* understanding of, and perception of God."

ৎৎ৵

A Question About God

As a spiritual seeker, the important question for you is not: *"What is god?"* It is: *"What stimulates my personal experience of God?"*

❧

The Truth About God

*W*hen you only have a collection of *ideas* about the spiritual realities, you can wonder: "Which of the many ideas created by humans present the *truth* about God?" When you *feel* the extraordinary perfection and love of God, there is no confusion. You *know* that you are feeling the truth.

৩৯৶

God Love

*I*f you wish to try a creative way of imagining what *God* is, then imagine God as *an extraordinary celestial love experience* that permeates all that exists. As you do that, remind yourself that this Divine reality lives within *you, always.* You only need to practice turning your awareness toward it to feel its all-loving presence in your heart.

৵৵

Your True Self

*M*any people feel: "My *feelings* are reality. I am the feeling that I am experiencing." But, that is only a momentary subjective experience, not the truth. You can affirm the *real* truth by saying: "I have an inner center of Divine perfection within myself. The rest is shifting sand, blowing in the wind. My *true self* is like a brilliant diamond, steady, pure, and extraordinarily beautiful."

&c∾

Divine Companions

*T*he God Consciousness did *will into being* certain companion beings to itself. *Your soul* is one of those Divine companions, continually rejoicing in a limitless existence of *perfect love,* shared with all beings.

৩৵

Accepting Dark Clouds

*W*hen you look at your present life on earth, you usually do not see perfection in every moment. At times, it may even be difficult to see some goodness. Accept that as an aspect of your human experience. It is as though you live in a beautiful green valley. You love the sunshine. Occasionally, there are dark clouds and a storm. You do not say, "I must move from this place." You accept an occasional storm as the price that you pay for living in that beautiful valley.

❧

Light In The Darkness

*E*ven in the midst of dark despair there is Light. Close your eyes and let your soul illuminate your inner vision. If at first you cannot see the Light, in time, the dawn of each new day will bring with it that Light and a promise of a new beginning.

ço¢

Joy In Life

One of your important purposes for coming into human form is *to find joy in human life on earth.*

෨ඏ

Power Over Your Thoughts And Feelings

*I*n your thoughts and feelings, *everything* is changeable. *You have power over your thoughts and feelings,* even though at times you may not feel that power. *The power to create thoughts and feelings is always yours to use as you wish.* How you use that power builds the ongoing attitudes and beliefs by which you live your life.

༜

The Truth

*A*s you manage the complexities of the world that you need to live through each day, always find time to remember the *truth*, even when you cannot *feel* it. The truth is: *You are an eternal soul, temporarily living a unique human life on earth, and you are always connected to God, and to the many souls who love you.*

കരു

Individualization

This is an era of *individualization* on earth. One spiritual teaching will not be perfect for every single human. Because of the tremendous diversity of human experience and knowledge that has unfolded through the ages, there are now many *philosophies, religions, beliefs,* and *approaches to awakening to the Divine.* Therefore, your personal challenge is to choose what inspires *you* on your own spiritual path.

༄༅

Your Personal
Spiritual Journey

*I*n the *beginning* of human life on earth, *you* were alive, living in a way that set into motion *a personal evolutionary process.* Your *present life* is another important step in that process that is leading toward a mastery of human existence in the physical realm. This mastery will bring about a profound merging of the human and the Divine in your experience, thus *completing your personal spiritual journey that was set into motion in the beginning of time.*

ৡৣ

Your Past Life Abilities

You are living your *present* life in a way that has to do with many important *personal accomplishments, talents,* and *abilities* that you achieved *in your past lifetimes* on earth. Even though much of that lives in you *beneath* your conscious awareness, it is all being brought into your present life by your soul as *patterns* to be built upon and *expanded* in your ongoing process of mastery of the human world.

છ∞લ

Your Free Will

One of the great gifts that God has given to humans is *free will*. How you as a unique individual choose to use that free will is *your* gift to humanity.

❧☙

Transforming Earth Life

*Y*our willingness to merge your human self with others through kindness, compassion, and love becomes part of a great *transformational force* that is now growing around the earth. As more and more people live that idealism, *it becomes the powerful force that will heal the divisions and separations caused by human selfishness.*

స్తిం

You As A Teacher

*A*s you become a one who understands the *cosmic interplay* between the *human* and the *Divine* in life on earth, and you *live* your understanding in your relationships with other people, you become a *teacher* to those who have not yet awakened to their own Divine nature.

ৡৡ

Manifesting The Divine

*I*n order for there to be *the manifestation of Divine Perfection in the earth realm,* it must come from humans *choosing* to use their *will* to express goodness and love in the world. *Human choices made in love open the way for remarkable transformative manifestations to occur on earth.*

✣

You And Your Soul

*Y*ou are your soul right now, in this moment. Although it can be difficult for the human mind to imagine this, right now, while you are temporarily experiencing yourself as a human being inside your physical body *within* time and space, you are *simultaneously* existing as your soul in a perfect, non-physical, spiritual realm *beyond* time and space.

৯৶৹

Your Personal Understanding Of God

A focus upon God can be a very important area of understanding for you, if you can comprehend God in your own *personal* way. You are free to release any teachings about God that you have absorbed from others that do not touch your mind and heart. Then, you can come to *feel* God through your daily spiritual practice. That way, your understanding of God becomes *your own,* not someone else's.

ৡৢ

The Path Of The Masters

*T*o worship *God*, but to avoid *people* because they might be difficult to interact with, will confuse you on your spiritual pathway. If you are willing to bring together kindness to people, *and*, a love of God, you will be walking the path of the Masters.

တွာ

Creating Love

Say to yourself each day: "I have the power to *create* love through my own thoughts and feelings. How will I use that power today?"

ত৵৵

Empathy And Compassion

*D*o not be afraid to *feel* the pain and suffering of another. If you have the courage to share their pain, it will stimulate a profound *empathy* and *compassion* in you that will uplift both of you as you help them through their healing process.

৩৵

Healing Negativity

*H*uman actions taken on selfish impulses, without regard for other people, *are the cause of human negativity. Kindness, compassion,* and *love* are the powerful forces that can *heal* human negativity.

&

Renewing Hope

*I*f you become discouraged about the state of
the world as it appears that the negativity is
increasing, remember that if you create *a deep love
of life and of humanity*, you will *renew your hope.* That
will free you from the discouragement that you feel,
and then you can stir in your heart *a longing to bring
forth inspiration and upliftment in order to help trans-
form the negativity.*

৯৵

Music And Meditation

As a refreshing change in your meditation practice, you can use inspiring music to help deepen your spiritual attunement. When human beings create beautiful music, they are emulating, in sound, the Divine Forces of God. Thus, music can help you create a mood of *loving expansion* and *holiness*. This can become a potent tool to use in some of your attunement periods.

❧

Inner Power

*E*ach day, you can address your outer circumstances in the world, and your relationships with other people, to try to create more of what pleases you. But, when you *cannot* change the outer world, remember that you *always* have the *inner power* to change your *attitude* and *to create thoughts and feelings of goodness, joy, and love.*

ॐ

Passion And
A Spiritual Practice

*T*he human capacity to become *passionate* about something is very great. You can become passionate about anything—your work, a relationship, a hobby. You can also become passionate about discovering your eternal nature. This can lead to a spiritual practice that can bring you some of *the most fulfilling experiences of your life.*

 క్ర

A True Love For Others

*I*f you can learn to sense the *goodness* within other people that flows into them from their soul, especially the people who challenge you, then you will know the *true* experience of love for other human beings.

৵৹৵

Teaching By Example

When you choose to live a spiritual life, you teach other people by *example*. They see kindness and love manifesting through *you*, and they learn that such expressions bring harmony and understanding to all people. Thus, *your presence as a teacher in the world becomes an important, profound influence in the healing of humanity.*

෨෮

Teaching Through Love

To be an inspiring teacher to others, it is not necessary to give them profound spiritual ideas, or to describe the workings of the universe, for those kinds of teachings *change* as the human *intellect* changes over time. What penetrates *all* human beings in *all* times are expressions of *love.*

৵৵

Serving Self Or Serving Others

While you are alive in human form, you are free to choose to ignore other people and lose yourself in your personal affairs, giving all of your attention to the satisfaction of your own needs and desires. However, when you come to the moment of your death, it will not be important to you how much you satisfied your own personal needs in this lifetime, but rather, *how fully you expressed your love into earth through your relationships with the human beings about you.*

৵৶

A Profound Truth

One of the deepest truths of life is: *Every moment of human existence, whether it is subjectively perceived as negative or positive by humans, is infused with the extraordinary energy of the Divine Love of the Creator.*

෴

A Spiritually Alive Experience

*I*n time, your meditation practice can become more than a ritual that you do by rote. It can become *a spiritually alive experience*. Such an experience *will cleanse your human perceptions* of the distortions caused by the negativity of pain and suffering.

॰੭ঔ৶

Applying Your Knowledge

*Y*ou alone have the responsibility for *applying* the knowledge that you gain in your life. *Acting upon your ideals* is one of the most important things that you can do in carrying out that responsibility.

৵৶

A Joyful Attunement

*M*aking an attunement should be a joy, a respite from the challenges of the world. If you occasionally find your present practice to be an effort, or a chore, experiment with new ways of retreating into silent moments. For a while, ignore your usual attunement method and use a new focus. If you believe in *the beauty of God*, then during your attunement, worship God. If you believe in the beauty of *humanity, idealism,* and *love,* then enter a silence and imagine a pure, pristine goodness that links you to everyone. Whatever you find to be *holy, good,* and *true* beyond the complexity of human affairs, that can be what you focus upon in your period of attunement.

ജ്ഞ

Your Focus

*W*hat you continually *focus upon* will appear in your life. If you keep your attention on beauty, you will see beauty. If you look for what is good in human beings, you will find that goodness. If you speak kind words and listen for truth, you will hear the voice of God.

৩৩

Your Soul, Your Companion

*Y*our soul is *constantly* loving you, never criticizing you or condemning you. Your soul walks every step of your human pathway with you. *You are never alone on your journey.*

❧

Demonstrations Of Divine Love

*T*hroughout the ages, enlightened spiritual teachers have presented humanity with examples of Divine Love *in the way that they lived* that went beyond the words that they spoke. Those ways of living were given as a *demonstration* to all of humanity of the pathway that leads to *healing human negativity,* and, to *mastering life in the physical world.*

৽৹৶

Fear And Trust

*I*t is at the moment of greatest fear that you need *the greatest trust in the Divine Creator,* and the Divine Love within you, so that you know that what you are fearing can never damage your *being.*

৩৹৫

The Uniqueness Of You

*T*he *uniqueness* of you as an individual human self becomes apparent when you realize that *your* particular thoughts and feelings *can occur only inside of you.* *Your* subjective experience cannot occur in another person. In all of the realms of life, there are no other realities that are *your* unique subjective human experience. That uniqueness tells you that something *miraculous* has been accomplished by the God Forces in order to make it possible that you are "one-of-a-kind" in all of Creation.

ॐ

The Physical Family

A deep mystery lies in the sense of *a physical belonging-together* that is shared by all living humans—a family sharing, being all of one family, one "body." *All* human bodies, in their *true, perfect, undistorted nature,* are of the same Divine *form* and *substance.* They all partake of the same Divine Forces that infused themselves into human bodies in the beginning of time.

৯৩

Angelic Beings

*A*ngelic beings are all around you. In the *physical* world, you will know that they are present through the kindness coming from other people. In your *inner* life, you will know that they are present by an inner whisper that quickens your heart when you most need inspiration and love.

৵৹৹৶

The Path Of The Masters

*Y*ou, in your inner being, are never at the mercy of life's situations. The power to *choose* how to *think* and *direct your attention* is a God-given gift. When you truly understand this power, and utilize it fully, you will find yourself *walking the same path that has been traveled by the Masters throughout the ages.*

ço∂

Pain And Your Commitment To Love

At times, *pain* can overwhelm all of your thoughts and beliefs about goodness. The negativity and darkness can seem to completely swallow you. Yet, with courage and trust, there can always be a return to *the commitment to love,* so that even the most extreme pain cannot destroy that commitment.

૭∼૨

Where The Divine Meets The Human

*A*s you deepen your spiritual practice, you will come to realize that the "place" where the Divine meets the human is *inside you.* It is *at the core of inner goodness* that lies at the center of your human *self.* That is where *the perfect energies of God* sustain you throughout your life. That is where you can experience *your eternal being* that can never be damaged or diminished.

ക

The Human Condition

*A*s you become more enlightened through your spiritual practice, you will gain a deeper understanding of *the human condition*. You will clearly see the human choices that create the darkness of negativity, and, *you will know how to bring light into that darkness* for the people around you to help them make different choices.

≫⟨

Divine Goodness

*D*ivine Goodness cannot be *imposed* upon humans living on earth. It is *prepared* by God and the souls, but it needs to be *chosen* by living humans through their *will*.

❧

Time And Timing

*I*n the *spiritual* world there is no *time*. In the *physical* world, *timing* is everything.

಄ঌ

Guiding Souls

*M*agnificent Divine Guiding Souls work with you continually, moment by moment, *beneath your conscious awareness.* Through your commitment to personal and spiritual love in your daily life, you can become *aware* of the love that those helping souls are pouring into you.

෨ၹ

A Matter Of Being

*I*n your meditation practice, learning to experience spiritual realities is not a process of forcefully eliminating obstacles to achieve a *result*. It is not a process of *doing,* or *working* at meditation. It is a matter of *creatively adjusting your inner perception* so that you can achieve a new kind of *experience*. It is a matter of *being*. It is a new, deeper way of *being yourself.*

౪౨

Living Kindness, Compassion And Love

*I*t is not enough to simply *know* about kindness, compassion, and love. You need to *experience* those feelings within yourself, and then *live* them in your life *until they are overflowing from yourself to other people.*

~

Staying Inspired In Troubling Times

*T*o stay inspired when you are worried about negative human affairs in your outer world *that you can do nothing about* takes an act of personal *will*. You need to use your will to turn your attention away from the *temporary* things that are troubling you that are beyond your control. Then, you need to remind yourself of what is *permanent* and *true*. You can do that by saying to yourself: "In spite of any temporary appearances of negativity that I see in human affairs in the world, *the forces of the Divine continue to permeate **all** human beings. We are all eternal souls, and nothing can damage our true being. Nothing can break the spiritual bonds that unite us all.*"

ℰↃℰↄ

The Pure Light Of God

*T*he pure light of God flows into your human self. Through the prism of your *heart* and *mind*, that pristine light is transformed into a vibrant rainbow that becomes your life.

∽∾

New Beginnings

*E*ach day is a *new beginning*. With the rays of the rising sun you are washed clean and you can start anew in your determination to create *goodness* in your life.

సాల

Healing Divisions Between People

When you are willing to *release your criticism and condemnation* of other people, you are healing the patterns that breed conflict and hatred in the world. That opens the way for the expression of *kindness,* and kindness *will heal the divisions between people.*

ভ

Inspiration Through Nature

*W*hen you are feeling mired in the daily challenges of the physical world, take a moment to focus your attention on something beautiful in *nature*. Man-made objects, although they can be beautiful, are only a *reflection* of the Divine. It is easier to feel the Divine through nature because it is *a direct creation* of the God Forces.

৵৹৶

Challenging People

When you feel frustrated and angry with challenging people in your life, remember that the same Divine Goodness that lives in you *also lives within them,* in spite of the fact that you do not like some of their choices and behaviors. Remember that, just like you, *they are trying to find goodness in their own way.*

❧

The Power Of Kindness

*K*indness may seem to be a simple thing, but it is great enough *to make manifest Divine Energy* in the physical world.

৩৽৻

The Cycles Of Existence

*N*ature is constantly demonstrating the ongoing *cycles* of earth existence. From the rising and setting of the sun, and waxing and waning of the moon, to the ongoing regeneration of seeds, the cycles of Nature are sustained by an invisible Divine energy that never diminishes. Why, then, would the cycles of *your existence as a human* be any different?

❧

Loneliness

*T*here would never be *loneliness* in earth life if everyone would remind themselves, with any human being that they encounter: "This person before me is *an eternal soul* standing in human form. Let me open my mind and heart to feel the preciousness of this soul."

৩৽৻৻

Becoming A Teacher

*B*y choosing to create *new* ways to see, under-stand, think, and feel, and by choosing to strive for a *larger* experience of life that goes beyond what appears in the physical world around you, you make possible the building of *a most beautiful spiritual structure* in your inner life. As that grows stronger, it attracts those who are in need of inspiration. Thus, through your own spiritual awakening, *you become a beneficial teacher to other people.*

ᕮᕰ

Separation

*H*umans create *separation*. They separate life into many categories, time into increments, distance into discrete spaces. This is possible because your present human self, in *its subjective experience,* can *temporarily* have an experience of being separate from all of reality. However, in the Divine realms there is *no* separation. Your soul lives within, and partakes of, *all* reality, and is joined to *all* beings.

తు___ఌ

Necessity

*I*n your daily *practical* life, at times *necessity* needs to take precedence over philosophy and theorizing If you are in a situation in the outer world that is challenging, try to change the situation before you turn your attention to your inner life. Then, remind yourself that even though you are having a negative experience, *you are an eternal soul. That negative experience cannot damage your being.*

వచ్

Imagining The Truth

*T*here is *never* a moment in your life when you are alone. Divine beings are always *with* you. They are always *loving* you. When you cannot *feel* that love, you can comfort yourself by *imagining* it, for indeed you will be imagining the *truth*.

৵৵

Sleep And Your Soul

*W*hen you go to sleep you are untying the knot of your ordinary human consciousness. As you fall asleep, if you turn your attention to the Divine realms, you will slip more easily into the welcoming arms of your soul, resulting in a more restful and more rejuvenating sleep.

ഗ∘ഏ

Purpose And Destiny

*I*f you believe that you have a specific *purpose* or *destiny* in life that has been *predetermined* by your soul, or by God, and you are waiting to find that before you can be happy, you could have a long wait. Your soul has given you *many* talents and abilities that you have achieved in your past lifetimes, but, *your soul does not force you to choose one of those as your particular path in life.* Your soul asks you to use your *free will* to decide which of those talents are important to you. Then, by acting on and expressing the ones that you choose, you can *create* the experience of *purpose.* As you achieve *experiences of purpose* by boldly making your own choices about what to do in your life, *you create your own "destiny."*

ɔ∽ɔ

273

Your Holy Temple

*W*ithin your physical body there is your human *self*, which is the meeting place of the human and the Divine. Thus, *your body becomes the holy temple of God.* If you treat your body like the Divine manifestation that it is, then it can become a more wonderful and marvelous vehicle for your earthly journey.

෴

The Present Moment

*Y*our life on earth is but a blink of an eye in the eternal scheme of things. When you gulp your life experiences too quickly, you *speed up your perception of time,* and, you can accelerate the sense of moving too quickly toward death. Take some time each day in the silence to *slow time* by pondering the deeper questions of life, and *by savoring the richness of the present moment.*

৽৽৽

Abundance Of Love

*T*he abundance of *love* that you create in this lifetime will be taken through the door of death into eternity and returned back into human life *magnified* in each new lifetime.

୨୦୧

For information about the work of
Dr. Ron Scolastico, go to:
www.ronscolastico.com

For The Greatest Good

*I*f you have a day in which you have trouble *remembering* the truths that you have learned, and you are not sure what you need to focus on during the day for the *greatest* good, here is what to do: Focus on *giving kindness, compassion, and love to yourself, and, to every person that you meet.* That is *always* a powerful way to guide yourself through any day in your life.

෨∞ல

Holy Ground

*I*f you are seeking holy ground, look under your own feet.

৵৹৻

Human Words

*H*uman words are spoken on two planes of reality. First, there is the *physical* plane in which words are intended to fall upon physical ears, and, therefore, to be understood by the brain and mind of human beings. Second, there is the *spiritual* plane in which human words carry *the energy of God*, resonating throughout the ages, falling upon the very fabric of time.

౪∞౪

The Veil Of Perception

Every human being "sees" and "hears" another through the veil of their own prejudices and expectations. So, do not worry about being misunderstood, for only you, your soul, and God can truly know your heart.

ക്ക

True Success

*S*uccess can be a very private accomplishment and often does not involve being recognized by the world. At times, living your ideals each day in a simple way, or being kind to someone who challenges you greatly, could be considered a personal success. At other times, success can be the achievement of grand and glorious things in the world. After your death, when you review your life, you will know what your *true* successes really were, and, *they will be the cause for celebrating and rejoicing in the soul realm.*

৩০৫

Forgiveness

*T*he act of *forgiveness* softens your heart and creates in you a receptive and welcoming demeanor. It is the bridge to *true understanding* between people.

ॐ

Transformation

*Y*our spiritual awakening can bring stimulating and fulfilling *changes* in your life. You can feel: "I am being *transformed*." You will realize that your transformation is leading you to illuminating new experiences that will make your life richer as you continue on your pathway.

৯৹

Your Relationships With Loved Ones

If your relationships with your loved ones are feeling too ordinary, or stale, you can use the following affirmation to re-stimulate your appreciation of those people in your life: "Here is a magnificent *eternal soul* who is now manifesting in my life as a loved one. This person is a remarkable being who has lived on this earth in many lifetimes, one who has done extraordinary things. *This is a soul that I will continue to love into eternity.*"

Extending The God Forces

*T*he kingdom of God is everything, including your human self. It began with a Divine manifestation of souls in the beginning of *time*, then diversified into many realms of consciousness, including the human dimension. In that human dimension, *you* are now *extending* the God Forces into earth by the way that you live.

৬৹৵৶

Choice And The Future Of Life

*T*he forces of God have made life on earth *possible*. It is the power of *personal human choice* that will determine the *future* of life on earth.

৯৯

Your Quest And The Unfoldment Of Human Life

As you learn to experience the majesty of Divine Love more and more, you will feel a vibrant and exciting *newness* in everything that you do, as if you have stepped into a thrilling new world of *beauty* and *magnificence*. You will feel such deep *purpose* and *meaning* in your life that each moment can seem to be part of an important *quest* that you have been on all your life. You will realize that *you* are truly playing an important part *in the unfoldment of human life on earth.*

ৡৰ৶

Your Power To Create Good

*I*t is a *miracle* that you are able to have the experience of being alive as a unique human. Your human *self* is a miraculous *reflection* of Divine patterns created by God. Those patterns have been placed into you to enable you to create a life of *goodness* on earth. To inspire yourself to accomplish this, say to yourself each day: "**I have been sent into life on earth to experience the goodness of *joy* and *love*. In this day, I will use my God-given power of free will to *create* that goodness.**"

৩৵৵

Your Spiritual Experience

A spiritual experience can be different for each
person, but, after you have enough practice in
opening to the spiritual realm, you can expect
some of the following qualities to be part of your
spiritual experience: Feelings of extraordinary *bliss*
and *ecstasy*; experiences of the most profound *love*
for all beings; a deep sense of the *holiness* of life; a
vast feeling of universal *oneness* and *harmony* with
all existence; and, eventually, *a transforming direct
encounter with the perfection of the all-loving God of
life.*

৵৵

The Highest Stage
Of Enlightenment

*I*n the *highest* stage of enlightenment, *your human self energy structure* can be elevated to such a greatly refined level that *it emulates and echoes the perfect Divine energy structure of your soul, and you powerfully shine the forces of God out into the world for everyone to share.*

৵৹

Four Keys To Mastering Life On Earth

*A*s a final reminder, here are the four keys to *mastering* life on earth:

- ✆ **Heal your feelings of fear and negativity.**
- ✆ **Love your own human self.**
- ✆ **Open your heart and bring forth kindness, compassion, and love from within yourself to share with the people in your life.**
- ✆ **Awaken to the eternal love of God that is always within you.**

When these keys are *fully* lived by you, *you will complete your earth adventure in the most magnificent way.*

శాఒఅ